W9-CIA-651

DADDY'S
LITTLE
Princess

DADDY'S
LITTLE
Princess

Taylor Made Publishing, LLC
PO Box 20245 Greenville, NC 27858
www.taylormadenc.com

copyright # 1-2120277461
ISBN: 978-0-9905225-5-3
Editor: Jorge L. Hernandez
Printed in China.

Dedication

MY DADDY AND I WROTE THIS BOOK BECAUSE WE WANTED OTHER LITTLE GIRLS TO BELIEVE THAT THEY CAN BE PRINCESSES EVEN IF THEY ARE WHITE OR BROWN OR LIGHT BROWN OR INDIAN. ALL LITTLE GIRLS ARE PRINCESSES. I WASN'T SURE I WAS A PRINCESS BECAUSE I DIDN'T SEE WHO THAT LOOKED LIKE ME WHEN I WAS YOUNGER. I THOUGHT BECAUSE I AM BROWN THAT I WASN'T A PRINCESS, AND THEN MY DAD SHOWED ME THE REAL PRINCESSES FROM AFRICA AND GUESS WHAT...THEY ARE BROWN! TO MY SURPRISE, ON THE (COMPUTER) SCREEN WERE ALL KINDS OF PRINCESSES. I WAS WRONG. THERE ARE CHOCOLATE PRINCESSES, AND I WANT OTHER LITTLE GIRLS TO READ THE BOOK AND LEARN ABOUT THEM, TOO.

MORGAN E TAYLOR

LITTLE MORGAN HAD LOTS OF DOLLS.

SHE HAD BIG DOLLS AND LITTLE DOLLS
CHOCOLATE DOLLS AND VANILLA DOLLS.
DOLLS OF ALL SHAPES AND SIZES.

HER FAVORITE DOLL WAS HER
PRINCESS DANA DOLL.

MORGAN ALWAYS WANTED TO BE A PRINCESS JUST LIKE DANA.

MORGAN'S DADDY ALWAYS CALLS HER HIS LITTLE PRINCESS.

THAT MADE MORGAN FEEL VERY SPECIAL, BUT SHE DID NOT BELIEVE SHE WAS A REAL PRINCESS.

"DADDY," MORGAN SAID, "I LOVE IT WHEN YOU CALL ME A PRINCESS, BUT I KNOW I CANNOT BE A REAL ONE."
"WHY NOT?" ASKED DADDY,

"BECAUSE <u>REAL</u> PRINCESSES ARE NOT CHOCOLATE LIKE ME. PRINCESSES ARE VANILLA LIKE MY DOLLY DANA."

WHEN DADDY HEARD THIS HE BECAME SAD, BUT THEN HE LOOKED AT MORGAN AND SMILED.

"BABY GIRL," DADDY SAID, "PRINCESSES COME IN ALL KINDS. HERE, LET ME SHOW YOU." DADDY OPENED UP HIS COMPUTER AND SEARCHED AFRICAN PRINCESS.

TO MORGAN'S SURPRISE PICTURES OF ALL TYPES OF PRINCESSES
SHOWED UP ON THE COMPUTER SCREEN.

THERE WAS PRINCESS ELIZABETH OF A KINGDOM CALLED TORO WHO WAS A BEAUTIFUL MODEL AND WAS UGANDA'S AMBASSADOR TO THE UNITED STATES.

THERE WAS PRINCESS AKOSUA WHO BECAME A FAMOUS ACTRESS HERE IN AMERICA. SHE PLAYED A LITTLE GIRL NAMED NETTIE IN THE MOVIE "THE COLOR PURPLE."

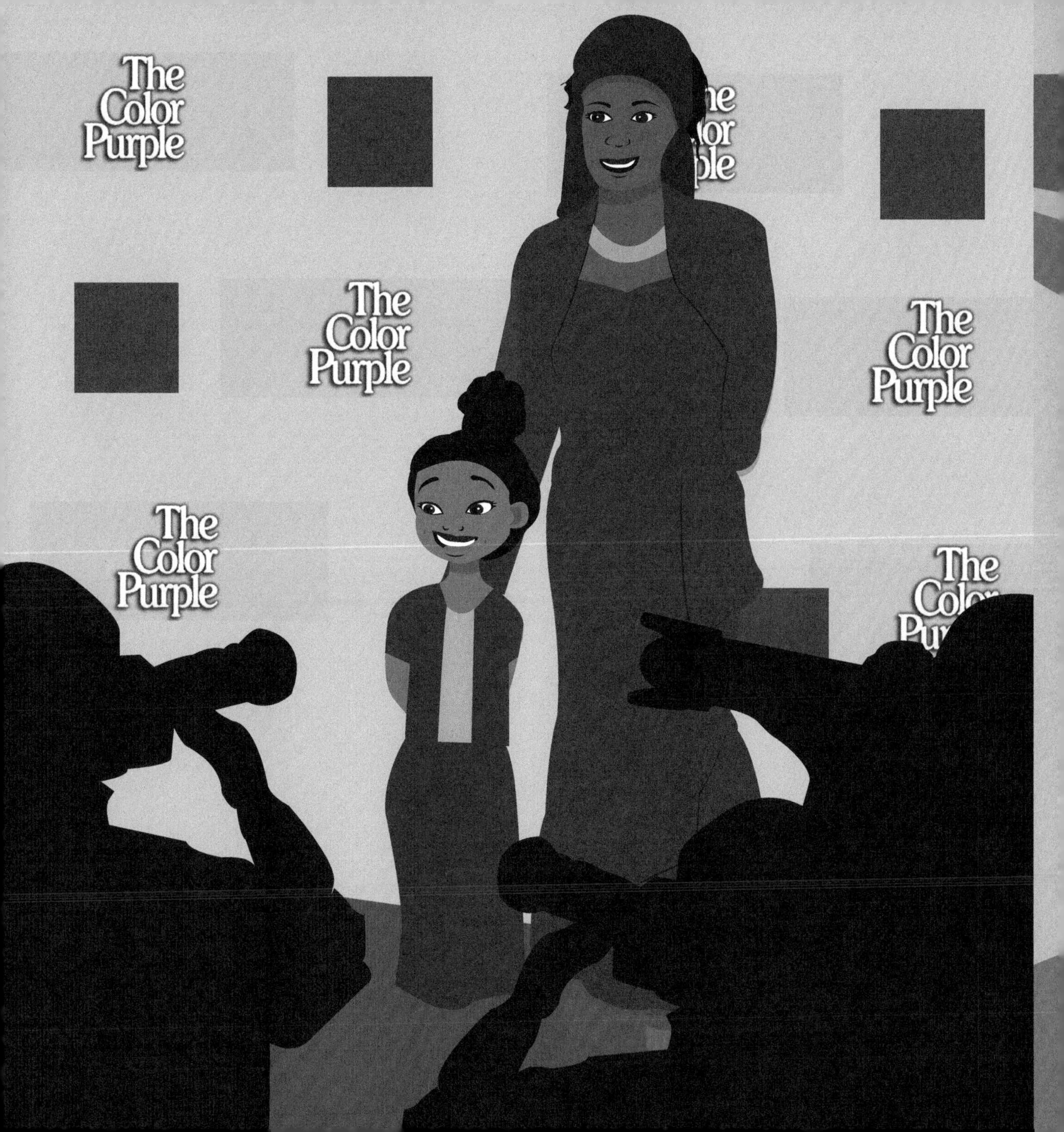

MORGAN READ ABOUT PRINCESS SIKHANYISO DLAMINI OF SWAZILAND WHO SPEAKS OUT SO THAT LITTLE GIRLS IN HER COUNTRY HAVE THE RIGHT TO BE TREATED FAIRLY.

MORGAN WAS AMAZED TO READ ABOUT SARAH CULBERSON, PRINCESS OF THE MENDE TRIBE IN BUMPE, SIERRA LEONE. PRINCESS SARAH WAS ADOPTED AND NEVER KNEW SHE WAS A PRINCESS UNTIL SHE GREW UP!

MORGAN'S HEART SWELLED WITH PRIDE AS SHE READ ABOUT THE POWERFUL QUEEN NZINGA WHO FOUGHT THE PORTUGUESE IN ORDER TO PREVENT HER PEOPLE FROM GOING INTO SLAVERY. THEY WERE NEVER ABLE TO CONQUER HER!

HER EXCITEMENT GREW AS SHE READ ABOUT QUEEN HATSHEPSUT, THE FIRST FEMALE PHARAOH OF KEMET (EGYPT). SHE RULED FOR MORE THAN 20 YEARS AND IS CONSIDERED ONE OF KEMET'S MOST SUCCESSFUL PHARAOHS.

PRINCESS AIDA DESTA WAS THE OLDEST GRANDDAUGHTER OF EMPEROR HAILE SELASSIE, THE LAST EMPEROR OF THE GREAT KINGDOM OF ETHIOPIA.

AND THERE WAS ONE PRINCESS WHO ISN'T A PRINCESS AT ALL BUT WHO IS ACTUALLY A KING. IN KING PEGGY'S VILLAGE THERE WAS NO NAME FOR A PRINCESS SO HER PEOPLE MADE HER A KING.

MORGAN'S EYES SHONE BRIGHT WITH AMAZEMENT. WOW, DADDY ALL THESE PRINCESSES ARE REALLY COOL AND THEY'RE BROWN LIKE ME. I GUESS I REALLY CAN BE A PRINCESS.

DADDY JUST SMILED AND SAID, "BABY GIRL, YOU ARE ALREADY THE MOST IMPORTANT PRINCESS IN THE WORLD. YOU ARE DADDY'S LITTLE PRINCESS."

KING PEGGY

PHARAOH HATSHEPSUT

AUTHORS
MORGAN E. AND G. TODD TAYLOR

PRINCESS SARAH CULBERSON

PRINCESS SIKHANYISO DLAMINI

PRINCESS AKOSUA

QUEEN NZINGA

ILLUSTRATOR
DELAYNA ROBBINS

PRINCESS AIDA DESTA

PRINCESS ELIZABETH

CPSIA information can be obtained
at www.ICGtesting.com
Printed in the USA
LVOW06s1058200716

496989LV00016BA/34/P

9 780996 593700